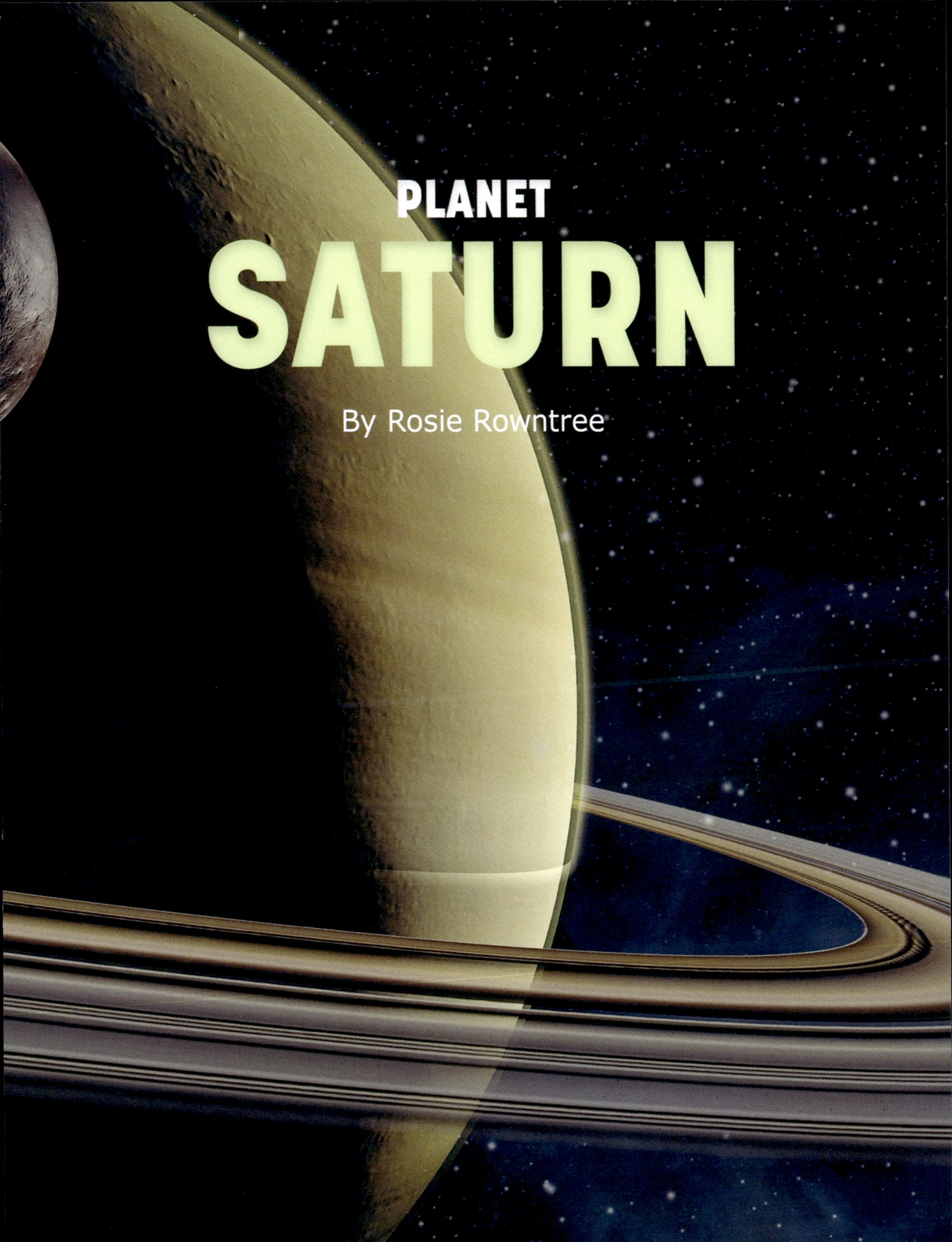

PLANET SATURN

By Rosie Rowntree

CONTENTS

First published in 2026 by Hungry Tomato Ltd
F15, Old Bakery Studios, Blewetts Wharf, Malpas Road,
Truro, Cornwall, TR1 1QH, UK.

Copyright © 2026 Hungry Tomato Ltd

No part of this publication may be reproduced, stored in a retrieval system, or transmitted in any form or by any means, electronic, mechanical, photocopying, recording, or otherwise, without prior written permission of the copyright owner.

A CIP catalog record for this book is available from the British Library.

ISBN 9781835696811

Manufactured in the USA

Discover more at
www.hungrytomato.com

Front cover image is an artist's impression of Saturn and two of its moons.
Title page image is an edited image of Saturn, its rings, and one of its moons.
Contents page image is an edited image of Saturn.

Words in **BOLD** can be found in the glossary.

WHERE IS SATURN?

Sun

There are eight planets in our **solar system**. The planets travel around the Sun. Saturn is the sixth planet from the Sun.

The time that it takes a planet to travel around the Sun is called a year. Saturn travels around the Sun once every 29 **Earth years.** This journey is called an **orbit**.

PLANET FACTS

Saturn is the second largest planet in the solar system. But it's very light for its size! That's because it is a **gas giant**.

Planets are always spinning. The time that it takes a planet to spin around once is called a day. A day on Saturn lasts for 10 ½ hours, compared to 24 hours on Earth.

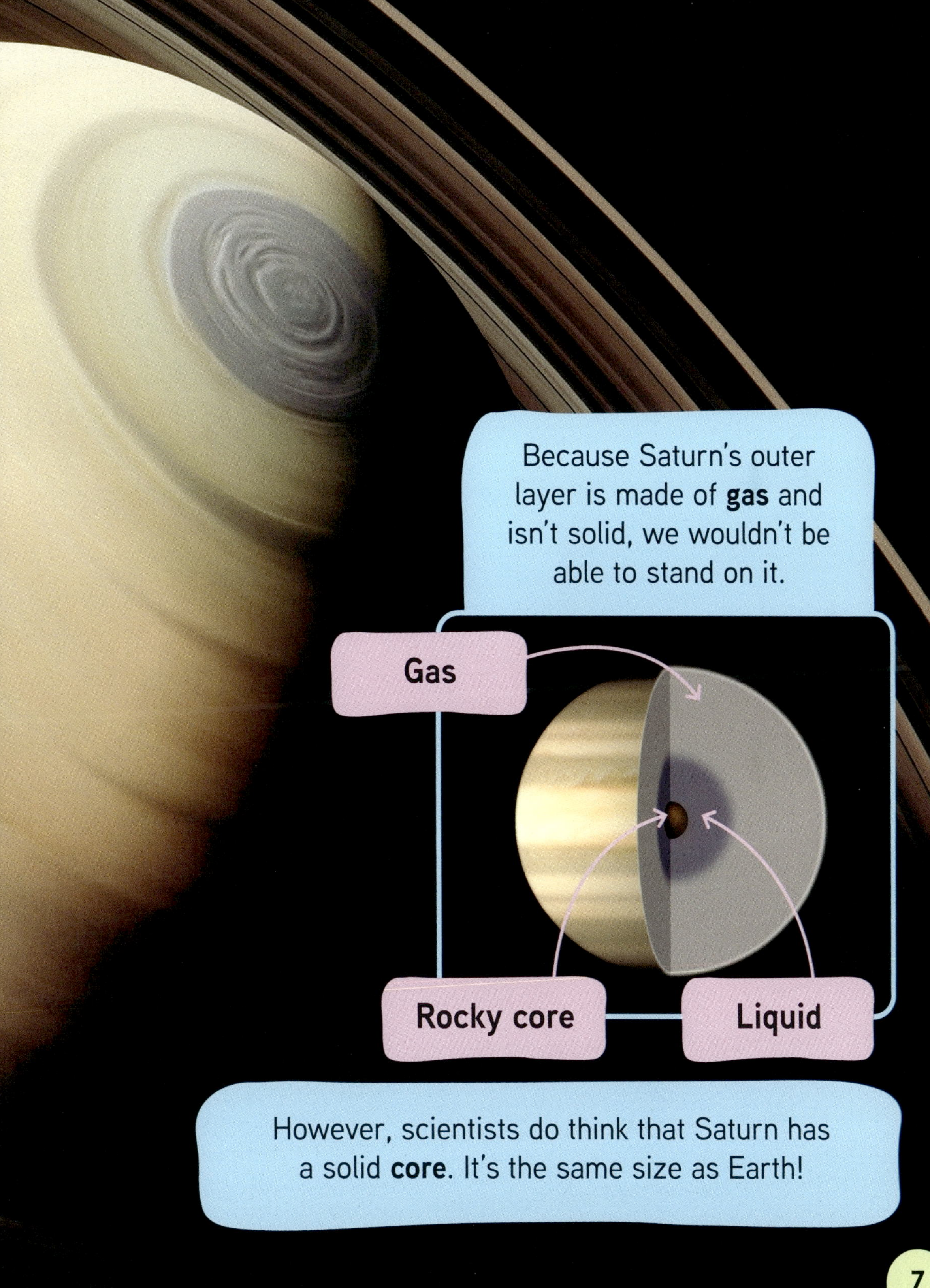

Because Saturn's outer layer is made of **gas** and isn't solid, we wouldn't be able to stand on it.

However, scientists do think that Saturn has a solid **core**. It's the same size as Earth!

WHAT'S THE WEATHER LIKE?

Saturn is a very stormy planet. It has "megastorms" that are like the **hurricanes** we get on Earth – except much, much bigger!

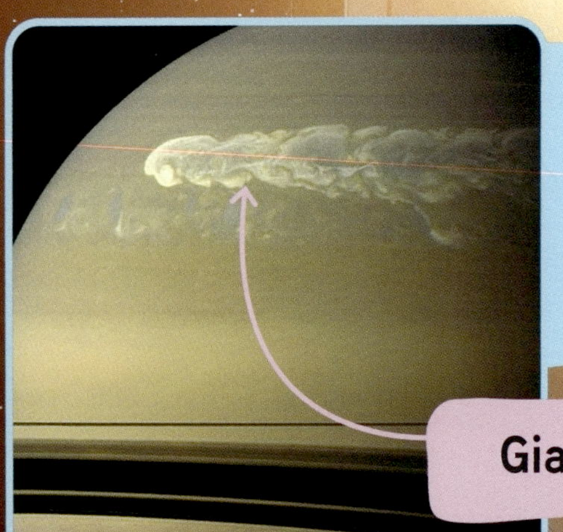

These megastorms look like big white spots. They only occur every 30 years, and scientists don't know why!

Giant storm

Another storm that happens on Saturn is called the Dragon Storm, because of its shape. It's a huge thunderstorm that creates lightning – just like a thunderstorm on Earth would do.

Dragon Storm

SATURN'S RINGS

Saturn has the largest and brightest rings of any planet in the solar system. They are mostly made of pieces of ice.

Some of these chunks are as big as houses! But most are very, very small.

There are seven rings in total around Saturn. However, some of them are very small and hard to see.

Scientists think that the rings were created when nearby **comets, asteroids,** or **moons** were torn apart by Saturn's **gravity**!
Saturn's rings

SATURN'S MOONS

Earth only has one moon – but Saturn has over 270! More and more are being discovered every year.

Enceladus is covered in ice and has the whitest surface of anything in the solar system. Scientists think that it has most of the ingredients needed for life!

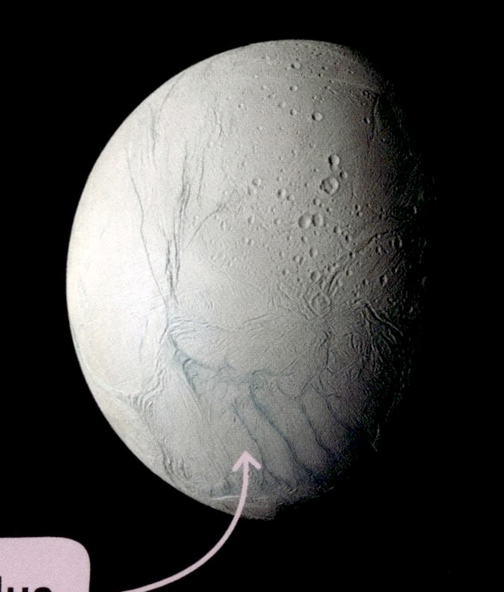

Enceladus

Iapetus is very strange because half of the surface is white, and the other half is a lot darker. The white half has lots of ice on the surface. Scientists don't know why the other half is dark!

OCEANS ON TITAN

Saturn's largest moon is called Titan. It's bigger than the planet Mercury!

If humans ever landed on Titan's surface, they wouldn't need to wear spacesuits! They would only need oxygen masks and lots of layers to protect against the cold.

It is the only place, aside from Earth, known to have lakes or seas of liquid on its surface! But Titan's lakes aren't made of water. They are instead made of gases that are so cold they have turned into liquid.

Titan is the only moon in the solar system to have a thick atmosphere.
Titan's atmosphere

FACT FILE

Only four spacecraft have made it all the way to Saturn. Despite this, scientists know a lot about this giant planet.

Saturn's rings are gradually disappearing! They are being slowly pulled into Saturn by its gravity and will be gone completely in a few hundred million years.

Because Saturn is made mostly of gas, it is very light. In fact, it is so light that if you could find a bathtub big enough, Saturn would float in the water!

Saturn's storms are not just bigger than Earth's – they're a lot more powerful too. Saturn's lightning is 10,000 times stronger than ours!

WHAT CAN WE SEE?

Saturn is the planet farthest away from Earth that you can see without a **telescope**. It appears in the night sky as a faint yellow star.

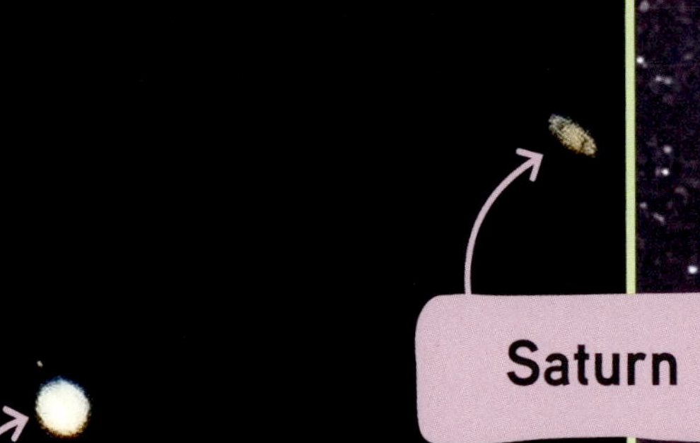

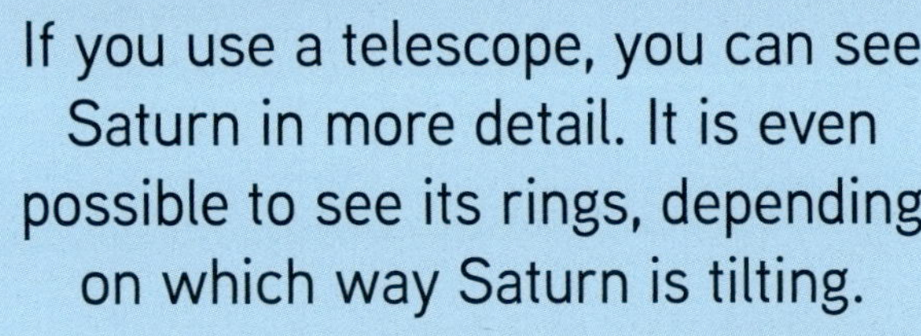

If you use a telescope, you can see Saturn in more detail. It is even possible to see its rings, depending on which way Saturn is tilting.

Saturn through a telescope

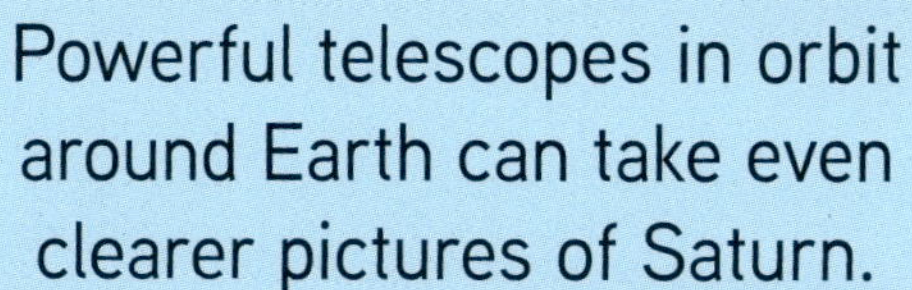

Powerful telescopes in orbit around Earth can take even clearer pictures of Saturn.

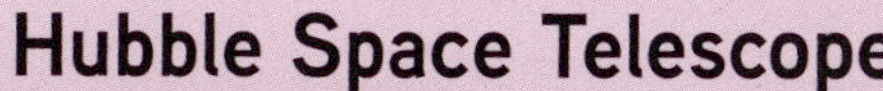

Hubble Space Telescope

The **Hubble Space Telescope** has used different filters to photograph Saturn and discover things that can't be seen with the human eye.

Saturn as seen through a telescope in orbit

EXPLORING SATURN

It took seven years for the Cassini-Huygens mission to reach its destination. It was made up of two spacecraft.

An **orbiter** called Cassini orbited Saturn to study the planet and its moons from a distance. It discovered two giant hurricane-like storms at Saturn's north and south **poles**.

Cassini

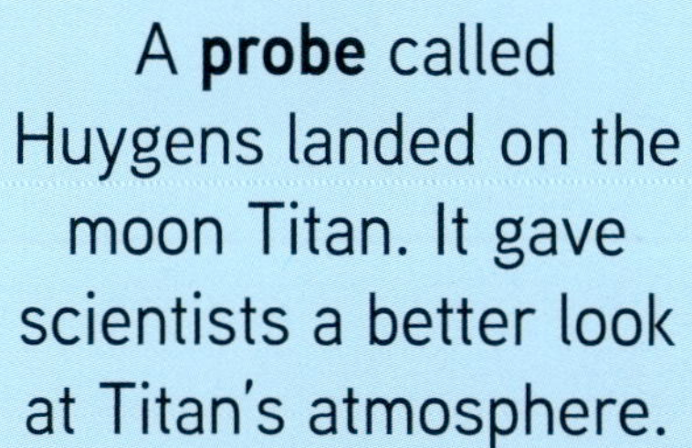

A **probe** called Huygens landed on the moon Titan. It gave scientists a better look at Titan's atmosphere.

Huygens

WHAT'S NEXT?

Two of Saturn's moons in particular have interested scientists for many years. They want to launch more missions to explore them in more detail.

Enceladus has liquid water underneath its icy surface. Some of this water bursts through into space. Future spacecraft would try to sample this water to see if there could be life living in these oceans.

Scientists think that Titan is similar to how Earth was billions of years ago. Learning about Titan could help us find out more about how our own planet developed.

GLOSSARY

Asteroids – small space rocks that orbit the Sun.

Comets – objects made of dust and ice that orbit the Sun.

Core – the middle of a planet.

Earth years – the amount of time that a year lasts for on Earth (365 days).

Gas – A substance that is neither solid nor liquid, and has no fixed shape. Many gases are invisible.

Gas giant – a large planet made of gases. Saturn and Jupiter are both gas giants.

Gravity – an invisible force that pulls things together. Gravity keeps our feet on the ground and the planets spinning around the Sun.

Hubble Space Telescope – a telescope in orbit around Earth.

Hurricanes – types of storms that have strong winds.

Moons – large, natural objects that orbit around a planet.

Orbit – the path taken by one object circling around another in space.

Orbiter – a spacecraft that orbits a planet or a moon but doesn't land on the surface.

Poles – the points furthest north and south on a planet.

Probe – an uncrewed spacecraft sent to explore outer space.

Solar system – the Sun and everything that orbits around it.

Telescope – an instrument that makes faraway objects appear bigger.

Picture credits:
(t=top; b=bottom; m=middle; l=left; r=right):

Wikipedia: By NASA / JPL / Space Science Institute - PIA08384: The Other Side of Iapetus, Public Domain 13br. NASA: images-assets.nasa.gov/image/0400741/0400741~orig.jpg 11tr; Images-assets.nasa.gov/image/GSFC_20171208_Archive_e002157/GSFC_20171208_Archive_e002157~orig.jpg 19bl; images-assets.nasa.gov/image/NHQ202012210002/NHQ202012210002~orig.tif 18tr; images-assets.nasa.gov/image/PIA06079/PIA06079~orig.jpg 21tr; images-assets.nasa.gov/image/PIA06197/PIA06197~orig.jpg 9br; images-assets.nasa.gov/image/PIA06254/PIA06254~orig.jpg 12br; images-assets.nasa.gov/image/PIA12320/PIA12320~orig.jpg 15tm; images-assets.nasa.gov/image/PIA12826/PIA12826~orig.jpg 8ml; images-assets.nasa.gov/image/PIA14922/PIA14922~orig.jpg 23tr; images-assets.nasa.gov/image/PIA18165/PIA18165~orig.jpg 19tr. Unknown 7br. Shutterstock: 42videography 16-17bg; Abriendomundo 18bl; Angel Soler Gollonet 10-11bg; Caludio Caridl 6-7bg; Dotted yeti 2-3bg, 24bg; Iva Foto 4-5bg; Joshimerbin 20-21bg; Jurik Peter 14-15bg, 22-23bg; SergeyDV 1bg; Vadim Sadovski 8-9bg, 12-13bg, 18-19bg.

Every effort has been made to trace the copyright holders, and we apologize in advance for any unintentional omissions. We would be pleased to insert the appropriate acknowledgments in any subsequent edition of this publication.